OVERCOMING DEPRESSION

BY

PASTOR DENNIS LEONARD

I would like to thank my *entire* staff. Their faithful love and support has helped bring this book to God's people.

I would especially like to thank Mark Grasmick, Paula McDonald, Linda McFann, Peggy McGinnis, and Marsha Saunar for their dedication to this project.

A *special* word of thanks to my wife, Joanne, for her ever present love and support.

Pastor Dennis Leonard

All rights reserved.
Dennis Leonard Publications

Copyright © 1992
by Dennis Leonard Publications
1301 South Clinton
Denver, Colorado 80231
(303) 369-8514

Contents

1. Discouragement Comes Against Us All 9

2. The Storms of Life 17

3. Keeping a Good Attitude 23

4. Words Affect Your Attitude 33

5. Praise Drives Out Depression 39

6. Things to Check 45

OVERCOMING DEPRESSION
by Pastor Dennis Leonard

INTRODUCTION

If you have joy in your heart, you probably have a healthy, successful, and joyful life. If joy is *not* present in your heart, you are probably discouraged, lonely, and depressed.

The Bible says, *"a joyful heart is good medicine but a broken spirit dries up your bones."* (Proverbs 17:22) You must get this Word into your heart and mind. God *loves* you, He has a *great plan* for you. Even though you may be going through difficult times today, you must believe that God is in *charge*, and He is working it all out.

The definition of depression is, a state of sadness, heaviness, or when someone is low in spirit and weighed down with the burdens of life. No matter who you are, sooner or later, depression or discouragement will affect you and come against you. Even the strongest of the strong, feel *down* or depressed from time-to-time. My prayer is that this book will help you overcome depressed times in your life.

Maybe you are single and you thought you would be married by now. Perhaps your business has failed, or the doctor has given you a bad report. Life has a way of delivering crushing blows. Most of the time, life doesn't work out the way we think it should; it can be depressing. Life can be full of hardships, difficulties, trials, tribulations, and even failures. However, no matter what your difficulties, you must realize that depression is your enemy.

You have a spiritual enemy who desires to "steal, kill, and destroy." (John 10:10) He has a trap set against you to cause depression to overtake you and make you think that your life is not worth living. That is why Jesus said, *"I came that they might have life, and might have it abundantly."* (John 10:10) In others words, you have a spiritual enemy who aligns himself against you, and his desire is to steal all your hopes, your dreams, and your purpose for living, so you will quit. When you feel depressed, all you can do is focus on yourself. Depression is the ultimate in *self-centeredness*. The enemy's plan is to make you withdraw and keep you isolated; thereby, causing feelings of depression to run rampant in your life. However, Jesus Christ, the Son of the Living God, came to give you the abundant life, and put the dreams back into your heart, that the enemy has stolen.

Anytime we suffer loss, no matter what that loss is, we are susceptible to depression. Maybe it's the loss of a spouse through death or divorce, the loss of a child, or a broken relationship. When you experience loss of any kind, it opens the door for depression to come in. Perhaps it's the loss of a pet, a friend, a job, or even the loss of money! It's depressing when you work hard and your money flies out the front door or through your fingertips!

Depression can be one of the most devastating emotions. I know from my own experience as a pastor, if depression stays long enough in a person's life, it can cause you to lose every reason for living. Depression will eventually remove every bit of joy from your life. You can reach the point that you don't care if you live or die. As a matter of fact, you'll probably wish you could die. Hopelessness is a lie from hell! If you feel hopeless, you've been fed a lie, because hopelessness is not for the child of God!

As many as one out of twenty people in America

suffer from depression. Many are being institutionalized. It's as serious as any major illness. If the cause is physiological, such as a chemical imbalance, your doctor needs to guide you. However, I am not talking about cases like this; I'm talking about a person living a life for God, and falling into depression.

Depression is usually a sign that something is wrong, either spiritually, physically, or mentally. For example, if there is something out of balance in your life spiritually, it is very likely depression will come upon you. When everything is right between you and the Lord, there is peace and life! **Where Jesus is, there is life!**

Let's examine the things we can do to overcome depression.

Discouragement Comes Against Us All
Chapter 1

"For even when we came into Macedonia our flesh had no rest, but we were afflicted on every side: conflicts without, fears within. But, God who comforts the depressed, comforted us by the coming of Titus." (II Corinthians 7:5,6)

We see here that the great apostle Paul was greatly discouraged. He was afflicted on every side. It doesn't mean that he was sick, it means there were great persecutions all around him. If you are a servant of the Most High God, then you have great afflictions and persecutions all around you. That's just the way it is. The Christian life is a life of conflict because this world is not our home; we are simply passing through.

The apostle Paul had many great conflicts in his life, he even had fears within. When persecutions come, fear rises on the inside of us; a fear that things aren't going to work out, or we're going be destroyed. Pressure had come against Paul, and he was depressed and greatly discouraged; but, in II

Corinthians 7:6, it says God comforted Paul by sending Titus to him.

No matter who you are, no matter how often you pray, you can become discouraged from time-to-time. In this day and age, we all have many opportunities to get discouraged. Life has a way of delivering crushing blows on a daily basis. Maybe you feel crushed today under the weight of your problems. We all experience hardships, trials and tribulations, and we all experience failures. Maybe in your own particular life you have been the object of prejudice or an injustice of some kind. Whatever the case may be, we all have difficulties and hardships to go through in life. If you think you are just going to breeze through life without difficulties, think again.

Obstacles present themselves in our lives every single day. When you get out of bed in the morning, your attitude should be, "I wonder what I'm going to overcome today!" If you think for one minute that you live in a fair world, you are wrong. If you think life is going to be a bed of roses because you have confessed Jesus as Lord, you are crazy. Obstacles are a part of life. As long as you are alive, there will be obstacles to overcome.

The dictionary's definition of discouragement is, "to be disheartened or to take away one's courage." One who has courage says, "I'm fighting until I win!" A person who lives in discouragement throws-in-the-towel, and believes that things are not going to work out. The bottom line is, you are either operating in faith, or you're operating in fear. I am not saying that if you're really *living right*, discouragement won't come, because it will. If you're living right, discouragement is probably knocking at your door. Don't let it stay there! Begin to say, "Even though this obstacle is in my way, I'm not quitting until I win!"

When we are confronted with the enemy of *discouragement*, we are tempted to give up on God and throw-in-the-towel. We are even tempted to *give up on our dreams and goals in life.* **Don't you do it!** It's a lie from hell! The Bible says, *"...for in due season we shall reap, if we faint not."* (Galatians 6:9) There's a season for your victory, so *chill out!* Your season is on the way.

The enemy has a plan to make you think there is no hope in your situation, or that nobody has it as bad as you do! The enemy's plan is to hinder your relationship with God, so you will backslide. He wants you to feel sorry for yourself so you aren't worth a hoot as a Christian.

God is teaching you along the pathway of life to trust Him. You may not like what you see, but He's teaching you how to keep your eyes on the Cross and to trust Him. That's what giving your tithes, your first 10%, is all about. He doesn't want your money, He wants your heart. He wants to know if you will trust Him. If you *can't* trust God in your finances, how can you trust Him in any other area of your life? You must guard against discouragement when giving your tithes to the Lord. The enemy would say, "Tithing doesn't work. You gave your money to the Lord, and now you can't afford to buy that new dress or suit you want." We must remember tithing is like healing, it's not always a quick fix, it's a process. As you are obedient in your tithing, God's Word says, "*...and my God shall supply all of your needs according to His riches in glory in Christ Jesus.*" (Philippians 4:19) You cannot allow discouragement to interfere with your obedience to Christ.

I believe discouragement is the enemy's number one tool to try and cause us to turn from the Lord. You know we are all very impatient creatures. We want what we want, and we want it now! If things don't happen fast enough, we quit or we get discouraged. Are you aware that when the going gets tough, many people leave Jesus Christ? When the going gets tough, most people leave the **Cross**. When Jesus went to the Cross, **all** of His friends deserted Him. After His resurrection, He appeared to over 500 at one meeting. He told them to go and wait for the power, and only 120 of the 500 waited in the upper room. Don't be impatient, and don't let discouragement keep you from trusting the Lord.

Discouragement is a state of mind. It starts in the mind and says, "God is **NOT** going to do what I thought He was going to do." It believes the worst. Discouragement is nothing more than DOUBT AND UNBELIEF.

"We are destroying speculations and every lofty thing raised up against the knowledge of God, and we are taking every thought captive to the obedience of Christ." (II Corinthians 10:5)

That's why God tells us to destroy every lofty thing that's raised up against the knowledge of God. When a thought comes to your mind, *judge it*. Is it in agreement with the Word of God, or is it against the Word of God? The battlefield is in your mind. You may *feel* like nobody loves you, but that's not true because it's against the Word of God. It is a lie. You must take your thoughts captive to the obedience of Jesus Christ in order to overcome discouragement.

When a thought comes in that's against the knowledge of God, you must resist and refuse it. There's an old saying that says, "You can't help it if birds fly over your head, but you can keep them from building a nest in your hair!" That means you may not be able to avoid stupid, crazy thoughts from coming in; but you can keep from entertaining them, and you can resist those thoughts and throw them out! Let's say you are walking down the street and you have a real nice hairstyle. Suddenly, a bird lands in your hair and tries to build a nest. What are you going to do? You will say, "Get out of here, get out of my hair!" You must do the same thing when thoughts of discouragement or depression come into your mind. Say, "Get out of here!"

The voice of the enemy is always trying to discourage you and take away your courage. He plans spiritual strategies against all of us. The bottom line is, if he can keep discouragement in your life, you won't be worth much as a Christian. You can't trust your feelings or your thoughts unless they are totally in alignment with the Word of God.

The three Hebrew children were doing everything right, and they found themselves in the fiery furnace! Ultimately, God is in charge of our lives. Sometimes God delivers us before we get in the furnace, and sometimes He delivers us in the middle of the furnace. It's God's decision. It's not up to us. He is in charge of our lives. We are the clay, and He is the potter. We are the workmanship of His hands, and He's molding us and making us. We may not like it, but we must be submitted to Him, and follow Him. Life is a series of conflicts. However, He's going to use those conflicts to mold, direct, shape, and make us everything that He wants us to be!

You might say, "Well, Pastor, I've been knocked down so many times, I don't know if I can get up again." Yes, you can! You belong to Jesus, you are a child of the King, and you can do all things through Christ who strengthens you.

One of the strategies the enemy uses against us is to convince us to quit coming to church. His whole plan is to isolate us, so he can destroy us. For example, when you take coals of a fire and separate them on your grill, in a matter of minutes those coals will go out. However, if you push them together, the fire will rekindle and the flame will burn hot. The same thing happens in church. If you separate yourself from the Body of Christ, you are setting yourself up to backslide and grow cold. The enemy plans spiritual strategies against you. He wants you to be offended at somebody or something in the church so he can isolate you and steal everything you have. That's why it's so important to walk in love and forgiveness. Keep your heart right with God, or you will be isolated and the enemy will destroy you.

Many things can happen in your life to discourage you. How *do* you respond when discouragement comes in? How fast you recover may depend on ignoring certain situations because you have no control over them. Your job, your marriage, and your family can discourage you. You must remember valleys are only temporary. God is working out a plan for your life. It doesn't matter who you are, your faith is going to be tested and challenged. However, if Jesus is on board your boat, you're going to make it to the other side!

THE STORMS OF LIFE
Chapter 2

TRUST GOD IN THE MIDDLE OF THE STORM

Don't let the storms of life leave you depressed. You must trust God in the middle of your storm.

"And on that day, when evening had come, He said to them, Let us go over to the other side. And leaving the multitude, they took Him along with them, just as He was, in the boat; and other boats were with Him. And there arose a fierce gale of wind, and the waves were breaking over the boat so much the boat was already filling up. And He Himself was in the stern, asleep on the cushion; and they awoke Him and said to Him, Teacher, do you not care that we are perishing? And being aroused, He rebuked the wind and said to the sea. Hush, be still. And the wind died down and it became perfectly calm. And He said to them, Why are you so timid? How is it that you have no faith?" (Mark 4:35-40)

The disciples were on the Sea of Galilee when a vicious storm came up. Jesus was taking a nap when the disciples said, "Go wake Him up!" Jesus awoke and said, "What's wrong with you guys?" They said, "Don't you see the storm? We're going to be destroyed." Jesus looked up and replied, "Oh, ye of little faith. Why are you so fearful? Don't you know, **I'm on board your boat!** I'm your Lord and Savior! Will you have some faith in me?" If Jesus is on board your boat, you're going to make it to the other side!

Do you know what was waiting for Jesus on the other side of the lake? The demoniac, who was filled with 6,000 demons! This storm came up to prevent them from getting to their miracle, which lay on the other side. Are you believing God for a miracle in your life? If you are, there's probably a storm trying to keep you from it. You must make up your mind that the storm is not going to stop you, regardless of what you see. If you're under spiritual attack, it's probably a sign that you are on your way to your miracle! Shout "Hallelujah!"

We do a lot of dumb things in our lives which bring storms upon us; however, we serve a God of **restoration,** One who loves us. He is not mad at us. He will take *all* of our mistakes and turn them for our good. No matter who you are, life is full of trials, tribulations, difficulties, and storms. There will always be opposition, just before your miracle comes. Every time a great difficulty comes into your life, start saying, "Oh, Jesus, what is it You have in store for me? The enemy sees something on the other side that I can't see, and he's trying to keep me from getting to my miracle." You must be determined to hang on to God!

If discouragement has come into your life, and you don't do something about it, it's only a matter of time until you throw-in-the-towel. Discouragement will come and steal every dream, and stop every miracle God has for your life.

Let me give you a word of *encouragement*. Your goals and dreams may be delayed, but they can't be stopped as long as you stay with the Lord. We must grow up in Christ. Mature Christians get discouraged, but recover quickly. Your maturity is evidenced by how fast you recover. Everyone of us has spiritual battles to fight. Things don't always go the way we think they should. However, as long as you hang-in-there with the Lord, He will cause you to *always* triumph in Christ.

"No weapon that is formed against you shall prosper; And every tongue that accuses you in judgment you will condemn. This is the heritage of the servants of the Lord..." (Isaiah 54:17)

Just because you are a born-again believer in Jesus Christ, does not stop weapons from coming against you; sometimes it increases them. Weapons are formed against you, no matter *who* you are. There's no sense in dwelling on it, meditating on it, or getting depressed over it. However, that same verse says, "and every tongue that accuses you in judgement will be condemned." In other words, even though you are accused of something you didn't do, you will eventually be found *not guilty*. If that's the case, isn't it pointless to get depressed? We must learn to trust God, even when the enemy tells lies about us.

God's Word says, this weapon, or lie, that the enemy has formed against you, *will not* prosper; it will not accomplish what it was sent to do. So, don't get depressed over it. Don't look at today, look down the road. My God will turn it for your good. So, **chill out**.

"A joyful heart is good medicine, but a broken spirit dries up the bones." (Proverbs 17:22)

You must make up your mind that you are not going to allow depression in your life. It is a destroyer and it is deadly business. Your confession should be, "Depression, you have no right in my life. I'm a child of God, and He's taking me to the other side!"

Depression is a thief. You must make a decision that you won't live in depression any longer. Take your eyes off yourself and begin to focus on Jesus! Your depression will leave as you keep your eyes on the *Problem Solver,* and not on your problem!

The root cause of depression is fear. It's a fear that things won't work out the way that we think they should. It's a fear of the past, the present, or the future. The bottom line is, fear and faith can't operate in your life at the same time. If you are operating in faith, you can't operate in depression. **Think about that!** Faith and fear are as opposite as the north and south poles. When depression controls your life, you believe that your situation looks impossible. Faith says, "My God is working it all out." Fear says, "All looks lost." Depression says, "Quit!" Faith never quits! Don't go by what you see; have faith in God.

"And without faith it is impossible to please Him, for he who comes to God must believe that He is, and that He

is a rewarder of those who seek Him." (Hebrews 11:6)

Make a decision today, to believe that God loves you, to believe He's going to help you, and to trust in Him. Dare to believe God and His Word.

Luke 4:18 says, *"The Spirit of the Lord is upon Me, because He anointed Me to preach the gospel to the poor. He has sent Me to proclaim release to the captives, and recovery of sight to the blind, to set free those who are downtrodden, to proclaim the favorable year of the Lord."*

He came to heal the brokenhearted and to set at liberty all of those who are oppressed of the devil. **Jesus Christ is the healer of the wounded.** Jesus is the One who is *your* substitute. He is the One who took *your* depression on Himself when He went to the Garden of Gethsemane. The pressure that Jesus felt in the garden was depression on His mind and soul. Will you let Him be *your* substitute today? Will you give Him every area of *your* life?

KEEPING A GOOD ATTITUDE
Chapter 3

As I was watching a television program recently, I saw people being institutionalized because they could no longer function as human beings, due to the sadness in their lives. We know difficulties happen in all of our lives. However, our attitude when dealing with those difficulties will determine how we come through them.

When difficulties come, if your attitude is "Woe is me, I am defeated, nobody has it as tough as I do," you will live a defeated life. If your attitude is right, however, you will say, "*I can do all things through Christ Jesus who strengthens me.*" (Philippians 4:13) Your attitude will determine how you come through the difficult times, trials, tribulations, tests or fires. Your attitude can even determine whether or not you come out of the trial or tribulation at all.

"*These things I have spoken to you, that in Me you may have peace. In the world you shall have tribulation: but be of good cheer; I have overcome the world.*" (John 16:33)

It does not matter who you are, or what religion you are a part of; if Jesus Christ isn't the source of your joy, life, and peace, you will never have *lasting* peace. Your peace is not predicated on how many sleeping pills you took to get through the night. Peace abides within you when Jesus Christ is the center of your life.

What is your attitude when trials come? Do you think that because you are a born-again believer in Christ, the storms are going to stop? If that's what you believe, someone has misinformed you. Difficulties, trials and tribulations come against us all! But, Jesus said, "Be of good courage. Don't let discouragement come in. Take your eyes off your circumstances, I have already overcome your trials and tribulations. You belong to Me, and I will bring you to victory."

We have all experienced *down* times in our lives. Jesus is saying, "Don't let life get you down. You are eventually going to win, if you're hooked up with Me." Jesus said, "You're going to have difficulties in your life. Cheer up now! It's only a matter of time, and victory will be yours." Your flesh will fight you. Your flesh is going to say, "See the circumstances in your life. You might as well throw-in-the-towel now." You must make up your mind whether you believe the Word of God, or the circumstances you see with your natural eye.

Storms come into *all* of our lives, but it's your attitude in the midst of the storm that determines whether you will have victory. If your attitude is one of discouragement, it will eventually **dry you up**, destroy your life, and land you in the pit of loneliness and isolation. The enemy wants to isolate you. Why do you think God said in Hebrews, *"Not forsaking our own assembling together, as is the habit of some, but encouraging one another; and all the more, as you see the day drawing near."* (Hebrews 10:25) Why do we come to church? We come to give honor to God, to bless and worship Him. However, when we assemble together, we encourage one another, and build each other's faith, while being encompassed in the corporate anointing.

If you are a child of the King, your attitude needs to be, I cannot be defeated, and I will not quit. I'm not talking about a magic formula, or about seven-steps-to-victory. I'm talking about knowing in Whom you trust. I'm talking about standing on the Word of God and the Rock of Christ Jesus. It's not a matter of a magic saying or my faith being in my confession.

You must know who you are in Christ; and know that He is the Lord of all, and He will turn everything for your good!

If you know who you are in Christ, you won't quit. The truth of the matter is, we are children of *The King*, not children of a beggar. We need to quit acting like we're beggars. "Oh, God, just a little morsel for me." We are children of the Most High God. The *Most High God* means that there is none other above Him!

"The righteous cry and the Lord hears, And delivers them out of all their troubles." (Psalms 34:17)

When you cry out to God, He hears you, so why are you going around saying, "I don't know why God *hasn't* heard my prayers." *"The righteous cry and He hears and delivers them out of all their troubles."* We live in an instant society and we expect God to do everything *right* **NOW**. However, God is in charge. He knows the end from the beginning. Does the Word say, "The righteous cry and He delivers them out of *some* of their troubles?" No! "Out of *all* of their troubles." So, chill out! If God says He will deliver you out of all of your troubles, why are you so discouraged and depressed?

Do you believe the Word of God? It says that "The *Lord is near to the brokenhearted, And saves those who are crushed in spirit.*" (Psalms 34:18) If you are depressed today, I want you to know that God is near to you. If things aren't going the way you think they should, remember, He's there with you and He is in charge.

"*Many are the afflictions of the righteous; But the Lord delivers him (us) out of them all.*" (Psalms 34:19) Translated from the Hebrew it reads, "many are the adversities of the righteous." Affliction is **NOT** *sickness*! The Word says, "Many are the difficult times, the persecutions, trials, tribulations, fires; many are these times, but the Lord delivers us out of them *all*." It rains on the just and the unjust. We know that as these difficult times or adversities come; Jesus is the crutch we lean on, the shoulder we cry on, and the One that will deliver us out of the fire.

Even though God's Word has told us that we are going to have adversities, He has also promised us that He will deliver us out of *all* our difficulties, trials and tribulations. I believe we bring many difficulties upon ourselves. However, God is able to turn every trial for our good. In the midst of adversity, God will use that tribulation in our lives to pull out judgmentalism, denominationalism, or the "bony finger" that we sometimes point at people and *their* sin. God doesn't *send* adversity. However, He can use it for our *good*, because He is a good God.

When you love Jesus Christ, it is only a matter of time before you see victory in your life. Be of good courage, He has already overcome the world! If you love the Lord today, then you can say, "My afflictions are many, but my God is going to deliver me out of them *all*." It's time to **chill out**, and begin to put your trust in the Master Potter.

Do you know why people commit suicide? They commit suicide because they believe their situation is hopeless. They believe that nothing is going to change, so they might as well end their life. **That is a lie from the pit of hell**, and it's contrary to the Word of God. If you know Jesus Christ, then you need to know that He will turn it *all* for your good. **Valleys are only temporary!** We're walking *through* the valleys. We're not staying *in* the valleys!

"*What then shall we say to these things, if God be for us who can be against us?*" (Romans 8:31)

Being born-again doesn't mean you won't have difficult times, and it doesn't mean that you won't have trials and tribulations come against you. It means that the weapons the enemy forms against you will **NOT** prosper. The Bible clearly tells us that there will be weapons formed against us. However, they will *not* prosper because of who you are in Christ Jesus.

"Who shall separate us from the love of Christ? Shall tribulation, or distress, or persecution, or famine, or nakedness, or peril, or sword?" (Romans 8:35)

"But in all these things we overwhelmingly conquer through Him who loved us." (Romans 8:37)

The Word tells us that in the *middle* of the storm, we are more than conquerors. Not because we confessed it with our mouth, or because of positive thinking. We are more than conquerors through *Jesus Christ* who loves us, and gave His life for us. Unless you know who you are in Christ Jesus, your positive confession becomes little more than words bouncing off the ceiling.

"For I am convinced that neither death, nor life, nor

angels, nor principalities, nor things present, nor things to come, nor powers, nor height, nor depth, nor any other created thing, shall be able to separate us from the love of God, which is in Christ Jesus our Lord!" (Romans 8:38)

What is your attitude when the storm comes? How do you respond? How do you react when you're doing everything right and the bottom falls out? Life has a way of disappointing us, but only **you** can make the decision whether you are going to live a joyful life, or whether you are going to have a contrite or broken spirit. Everyone sinks into depression from time-to-time. However, the Word of God tells us there is *NO* situation that is hopeless. The problem with hopelessness is your mind actually believes there is no way out. Your mind says, "This problem is so overwhelming, it can't be solved." You must remember there is nothing too big or impossible for God.

I think the saddest and most depressing times in my life, are when I know that I have paid my tithes, given offerings, I've been praying, I'm in the Word, and I believe I'm doing everything I'm supposed to do, yet it isn't working for me. The thought that continually comes to my mind is, "Why doesn't God answer my prayers? I'm doing everything right!" It is easy to fall back into *religion*. Religion says, "You must *earn* your miracle." God knows the end from the beginning, and we must trust Him and allow Him to be in charge. That takes not only *faith*, but *patience*.

It's time for each of us to change our attitudes about our difficult situations. You're either living in joy or in depression. Deuteronomy 30:19 says, *"...I have set before you life and death, blessing and cursing: therefore choose life, that both thou and thy seed may live."* **You** make the choice. Serve God and be blessed, or serve the flesh and be cursed. This is a choice only **you** can make. You can either choose to live with a joyful heart which is *good medicine,* or live in depression.

WORDS AFFECT YOUR ATTITUDE
Chapter 4

The words you say with your mouth affect your attitude. Be careful of the words that come out of your mouth. If your talk is negative, if you always talk about what the devil does, you're going to live a depressed life. Your words either fuel *faith*, or your words fuel *discouragement*.

Jesus said, *"Do you not understand that everything that goes into the mouth passes into the stomach, and is eliminated? But the things that proceed out of the mouth come from the heart, and those defile the man."* (Matthew 15:17,18)

In other words, you are not defiled by what goes into your body, you are defiled by the words that come out of your mouth. When you say, "I just can't believe this. Everything I touch fails. I'm so discouraged. Nothing works for me." You have just established your future.

"If you've been snared with the words of your mouth, (you) have been caught with the words of your mouth." (Proverbs 6:2)

The words you say will definitely direct your life. Your tongue acts as a rudder; it will guide your life just like a rudder guides a ship. I'm not talking about "name it and claim it." I'm not saying you should confess a Cadillac, and when you wake up, find one in your driveway. That's the spirit of greed. I'm not even talking about *positive thinking*, even though the *positive thinking* the world talks about was stolen right out of the Word of God and perverted! Our *positive confession* is the *Word of God*! The promises of God are "yea" and "amen." God's Word is *very* positive. If you'll say what God says about your situation, you'll be a very *positive person* and your confession will be *positive* as well. However, our faith is not in our confession. Our faith is in the **Word of God** and in **Jesus Christ** the Solid Rock.

There have been difficult times in my life, and when I started talking about my problems, they were soon blown totally out of proportion. When you talk about your difficult times, you'll eat the "fruit" of what you are saying. If you are living a defeated life, start by changing your words. What words would God have you say? The way you judge the words in your mouth is by asking yourself; if

Jesus were standing beside me, would I say this? "Oh, I just don't know if I can make it. I know that Your body was my substitute and You shed Your Blood for me; but I just don't think You are big enough to handle this trial in my life." Would you say that if Jesus were standing beside you? The Bible says that "... *the righteous man shall live by faith.*" (Romans 1:17) You must not go by what you see or what you feel. Rather walk according to the Word of God.

"*With the fruit of a man's mouth his stomach will be satisfied; He will be satisfied with the product of his lips.*" (Proverbs 18:20)

You will eat the fruit of what you are speaking out of your mouth. If you're always talking negative, you're going to end up with a negative, discouraged, and depressed life. If you're saying what God says about you, you'll eventually eat that fruit.

"*Death and life are in the power of the tongue, and those who love it will eat its fruit.*" (Proverbs 18:21)

Death and life are in your mouth. You speak death or you speak life with the words that come out of your mouth.

It is crucial that you remember, the attitude you have in the midst of the storm determines how you come out of that storm. Storms and difficulties are always going to come. The question is, what is your attitude in the *middle* of the storm? The words you speak out of your mouth will affect your attitude.

If you go by how you feel, you'll quit, and you'll be destroyed. You can't trust your feelings, unless your feelings line up with the Word of God. "Well, I just don't feel like God loves me." It doesn't matter how you *feel*.

Nothing can separate you from the love of God. *"Who shall separate us from the love of Christ? Shall tribulation, or distress, or persecution, or famine, or nakedness, or peril, or sword?"* (Romans 8:35) That's what the Word says. **NEVER** go strictly by your feelings! It is extremely important that every child of God realize the valleys are only *temporary*. Every storm will pass, the bad times will pass, and your victory is on the way.

We all have mountains to climb, and valleys to walk through, but you can't dwell on them. The more you talk about your problems, the bigger they become. When trouble comes into your life, start saying, "*Many are the afflictions of the righteous; But the Lord delivers him (me) out of them all.*" (Psalms 34:19)

The twelve children of Israel were sent out to spy on the Promise Land. Do you know that each one of them received what they spoke from their mouth? Ten of the spies said, "The giants are so big, there's no way that we can win!" However, two of the spies, Joshua and Caleb, came back and said, "The giants are big, but we can take the land! There's nothing impossible with our God."

Your words establish *faith* or your words establish *discouragement*. When you catch yourself saying the wrong thing, just reverse your words. Say, "Oh, I'm sorry, I didn't mean to say that." You must speak faith out of your mouth. You will either dig yourself a grave with the words you say, or you'll eventually dig yourself out of your problems, with the Lord's help.

I don't know what giants are in your life, but your giants are *nothing* compared to our God. Start confessing what God says about your situation. Start saying, I'm born of God! Victory is mine! I'm more that a conqueror through Christ Jesus who loves me! *"...in all these things we are more than conquerors through Him that loved us."* (Romans 8:37)

The truth of the matter is, God will turn every situation for your good, if you'll stay with Him. The enemy is always trying to get us to go back into the world where we came from. That's a lie from hell. God has a *victorious* plan for your life. Cheer up, and chill out!

We are the children of the Most High God. He has it *all* under control. What is your attitude right now in the midst of your storm? Your *attitude* and your *words* are going to determine whether you walk in victory or defeat.

PRAISE DRIVES OUT DEPRESSION
Chapter 5

When the problems of life come, I Peter 5:7 says, *"Casting all your cares (burdens) upon Him; for He cares for you."*

You have to learn, as a born-again believer in Christ, to cast your cares on God and not pick them up again. Human beings are not *equipped* to carry the pain and burdens of this life. Jesus came to be your burden bearer. He's the crutch we lean on, and the shoulder we cry on.

You must learn to give your problems to the Lord and say, "Lord I'm yours, and since You love me, I'm giving You these problems. I've done everything I know to do and I'm casting them on You." You have to learn to give your problems to Him and let Him keep them.

We love to take our burdens to the foot of the Cross. However, when we get up from our knees, we pick up our burdens, and put them right back on our shoulders. We must learn to trust the Lord! Somehow, someway, it's all going to work out. All our worrying, fretting, and stewing is not going to change a thing.

One way you can cast all your cares on Him, is by *living a life of praise.* Isaiah said put on *"...the garment of praise for the spirit of heaviness."* (Isaiah 61:3) Heaviness gets down in your spirit. Joy gets down in your spirit, as well. If you stay in heaviness or depression long enough, it will destroy you and steal everything in your life.

Praise Your Way To Victory

Praise separates us from all other religions. If you went to any religious temple, you wouldn't hear music, and see people clapping and dancing before their god. We are separated from every other religion, as born-again believers. Our God went into the grave, conquered death and hell, put His foot on Satan's ugly neck, took the keys of death and hell, and **rose up out of the grave victorious!** He is the only one who has defeated death! We can worship the way we do, because our God is *alive,* and our God's Name is Jesus Christ.

Paul said in Hebrews 13:15 to *"...let us offer the sacrifice of praise to God, continually."* Why do you think he called it a *sacrifice*? He called it a sacrifice because your flesh will fight you; your flesh will not want to praise God. You might feel you don't have any reason to praise God, and you *deserve* to be depressed! Nobody can put on the garment of praise for you. It is something *you* will have to do for yourself.

Psalms 22:3 says, "*O Thou who art enthroned upon the praises of Israel.*" Praising God brings His power into your life. God *inhabits*, or lives within, the praises of His people. No praise, no power. That's why praising churches see the power of God. Dead churches don't receive much from God. You should *NOT* stop praising the Lord just because you're depressed. In fact, when you are depressed, that's when you need to *crank it up*. You're waiting for God to do something in your life, and God is waiting for *you* to step out in faith, and begin to praise and worship Him. Get lost in praise and worship, and watch yourself come out of depression. Depression can *never* overcome someone who comes before the Lord in true praise and worship. When you mature in your spiritual walk to the point that you praise the Lord in the *heat of battle*, then you will know you're making progress. As you learn to praise God in the *battle*, you allow the battle to be the Lord's. He's the

Warrior, and praise puts Him in charge!

One of the best ways to get out of discouragement is to **praise your way out**. Paul and Silas were in prison at the midnight hour, (Acts 16), and as they continued to praise the Lord, their chains were loosed. The question is often asked, "How long should I praise God?" You praise Him until the chains have been loosed. Stop dwelling on your problems! Think on Jesus! Praise your way out! Discouragement says, "God has forgotten me. He doesn't care about me." *That's nothing but a lie.* When discouragement comes in, you can't dwell on it. Valleys are only temporary. Discouragement will pass; just wait it out. Praise Him until the chains of depression are broken off you.

If you truly trust the Lord, if you are truly walking by faith and not by sight, you will live a life of praise. In fact, you will realize that you won't *make it* unless you live a life of praise. If the enemy steals your praise, he'll steal everything you have.

I know you've heard this before, however, it is extremely important that you put this principle of praise into practice **NOW**.

Put on some of your favorite praise music, and get lost in worshipping the Lord. It will change your attitude immediately. Do it now.

Things To Check
Chapter 6

GET INTO THE WORD

If you find yourself in a depressed state, check your personal walk with the Lord. One of the first things your flesh wants to do when you are depressed, is to get you to put down your Bible, stop praying, and quit coming to church. If that's what you have done, you had better make up your mind to get into church where the corporate anointing can help set you *free*. You will have to make yourself do things that you don't want to do. When you maintain a daily relationship with the Lord, it helps remove depression from your life.

The Word of God will lift you out of depression when nothing else can. The parable in Mark 4:14 talks about four different kinds of people and their walk in life. When the Word is sown into people who are good ground, it produces a good crop. If they're not good ground, there isn't a good crop. In other words, the better ground you are, the more fruit will come out of your life. In fact, in Mark 4:20, it says that some will bear 30, some 60, and some 100-fold, depending on how good the ground is.

"The sower sows the word. And these are the ones who are beside the road where the word is sown; and when they hear, immediately Satan comes and takes away the word which has been sown in them." (Mark 4:14,15)

Your spiritual enemy is not in the least bit afraid of *you;* but, he *is* controlled and restrained by the Word of God. You will never see in scripture where Jesus said, "I bind you, devil." You won't find it in one single place. Since Jesus is our example, shouldn't we follow the Lord Jesus Christ? We don't follow man, we follow Jesus and His Word. Jesus said, "I speak the Word, and the Word will control you, Devil!" Now, if you want to bind the devil, that's fine. However, it's the *Word* that binds the devil, when spoken in faith.

The sower sows the Word, and the enemy comes to steal the Word. He's not afraid of *you*, and his objective is to get the *Word* out of your heart. When you come to church and the Word of God is sown into you, before you get to the parking lot, something might happen to try and steal the Word from your heart. "Can you believe the way they treated my children in Children's Church!" "Do you believe how noisy that guitar was!" "Can you believe the way that preacher acted up there!" Again I say, before you hit the parking lot, the enemy comes to try and steal the Word out of your heart! If you're *good* ground, you just throw that thing off. Remember, the enemy is after the Word of God that's sown in your heart, and he is trying to keep it from going forth.

We're talking about overcoming depression; a mind-set, an attitude of "I can not be defeated." Challenges are going to come in your life when you get a new revelation of the Word of God. The enemy will come to steal the Word out of your heart. What revelation have you recently received from God? (Healing, prosperity, etc.) The enemy continually tries to steal the Word that's sown in your heart to keep you from going on. If you have an area of revelation in your life, such as in the area of forgiveness, before the week is over, you will probably want to kill someone and repent later! Understand, when you are gaining new spiritual territory, things can get difficult. Don't let depression get you down. Don't let depression stop you! Depression and discouragement can keep you from going on with the new revelation you have in your heart.

GET RID OF ALL KNOWN SIN IN YOUR LIFE

It is so important to realize that *sin* causes *depression*. For example, if you willingly sin, then you feel guilt and condemnation, and you open the door for depression to come in. The only way I know to live guilt-free and without depression is, as soon as you realize that you have sinned, confess your sin and turn from it. Are you aware that our flesh likes to sin? Our flesh has a sin nature; it is very difficult to control our flesh. We find ourselves continually giving in to fleshly desires, which actually allows sin in our lives. That sin nature or carnality will allow depression to come into our lives as well.

The only way to remove depression from your life is, when you fall into sin, confess your sin and turn from it; which means "don't do it". If you slip and sin again, repent of your sin and turn from it again. You must repent and get right with God, then depression will not gain a foothold in your life. Depression will come against you if you *knowingly* sin and don't do something about that sin. God will deal with you in that area of sin if you don't repent. If you don't deal with your sin, depression will overtake you.

Check Your Forgiveness Level

Are you walking in unforgiveness towards anyone? If you are *not* walking in forgiveness, depression can come in. We are to live differently than the world lives, and that means that we must walk in love and forgiveness towards everyone, even those who have hurt us. Your life is no different from mine. We all are hurt on a daily basis, and we all have to walk in forgiveness on a daily basis. You must *check your forgiveness level*.

God tells us in Matthew 18:32-33, *"Then summoning him, his lord said to him, You wicked slave, I forgave you all that debt because you entreated me. Should you not also have had mercy on your fellow slave, even as I had mercy on you? And his lord moved, with anger, handed him over to the torturers until he should repay all that was owed him. So shall My heavenly Father also do to you, if each of you does not forgive his brother from your heart."*

In other words, if we don't forgive all those who have hurt us, He'll turn us over to the tormentors. One of those tormentors is *depression*. To walk in forgiveness is a major factor in walking free of depression.

FACE YOUR RESPONSIBILITIES

Don't be a procrastinator. Procrastination will cause depression. Here's an example: You know that you have a job to do, and you keep putting it off. The result is, anxiety builds and you become anxious. If you are not careful, depression will come against you. When you know that you have a task to do, ***don't procrastinate.*** I think it is a normal tendency for people to be procrastinators. "Why do it today if I can do it tomorrow?" This attitude, however, will create anxiety within you. When you know that you have something to do, ***do it!*** Face that responsibility.

GIVE OF YOURSELF

The last thing we want to do when we are depressed, is to give of ourselves to help others. Instead we want to wallow in self-pity and say, "Oh, look at my life. Nobody has the problems I have." We must get the focus off ourselves. Jesus said in Matthew 10:39, *"He who has found his life shall lose it, and he who has lost his life for My sake shall find it."* The problem with depression is it focuses strictly on self. *"I* am *so* depressed. *My* life is *so* miserable. *I* don't think I even want to get out of bed. *I* have no reason to live. Somebody help me, me, me. Nobody has it as bad as me, me, me."

Jesus said, "...lose your life for my sake, and you will find it." Somehow you need to get the focus off yourself, and begin to focus on helping someone else. *"Faith without works is dead."* (James 2:20) It is one thing to read this, and quite another to do something about it. If you don't put this concept into action, nothing is going to change in your life.

"Give, and it will be given to you; good measure, pressed down, shaken together, running over they will pour into your lap. For by your standard of measure it will be measured to you in return." (Luke 6:38)

If you want to live a good, healthy life, you *must* give of yourself to help others. If retired people get involved in doing something for someone else, they live full, productive lives. If they don't, some die within months after retirement. They have no reason for living, nor any purpose for life. You can be 20 years old, yet have no reason for living. If you are busy touching and helping others, you won't have time to dwell on your problems, or be depressed.

If you love Jesus Christ, and are serving Him, it

is only a matter of time, before He takes you to victory. You must learn to *"Cast all your cares on Him...,"* (I Peter 5:7) and wait out your storm, before you can get to the other side. Remember, Jesus said, *"...My yoke is easy and My burden is light."* (Matthew 11:30) If you are depressed and always down, you're not yoked up with Jesus, you're yoked up with the flesh. Get back to that loving relationship with the Lord, and life won't seem so difficult.

God's way is *to give it away*, and watch it come multiplied back to you. **Give of yourself.** Going to church on Sunday is good. However, it is nothing compared to what God will do for you, if you are involved in your church. Watch God do miracles in you, and release you from depression, as you give of yourself to help someone else. Give of yourself and watch God multiply it back to you.

You Must Learn To Put The Past Behind You

If you dwell on your past, you'll end up depressed. Even if you've failed God miserably, remember that you serve a God that loves you. He will always cause us to triumph in Christ Jesus if we hang-in-there with Him. You can't unscramble eggs! What's done is done! The past is the past! Of course you don't deserve His grace, but that's what grace is all about. You don't deserve His love either, but that's what God's love is all about.

Paul said, "...*forgetting what lies behind and reaching forward to what lies ahead, I press on toward the goal for the prize of the upward call of God in Christ Jesus.*" (Philippians 3:13,14)

It's time to put your past behind you. If you've asked the Lord to forgive you, then He's already washed it away, and your past is gone. Now you need to put it behind you and move on.

CONCLUSION

If you've come to the end of your rope, tie a knot and hang on. Paul said, *"Having done everything (you know to do), **stand**."* (Ephesians 6:13) You must stand until the hand of God changes your life or your situation. Difficulties will come and go, but you must stand firm in your faith, knowing the valleys and the storms will eventually pass. We are not strong in the power of our confession. We are *not* even strong in our faith, unless our faith is in Jesus Christ. We know, in the middle of the storm, "He's on board our boat," so there is nothing to fear. We are strong in the power of His might. If you are in a storm right now, you *can* have peace in the middle of the storm. Start saying, "This storm will pass." (Say it out loud)

Anytime we decide to do something for God, hindrances will present themselves. Discouragement will come against us as a result of the hindrances. You will probably want to quit. We all do! It's a natural feeling to want to quit. However, there's a difference between wanting to quit and actually quitting.

When you are a servant of the Most High God, your spiritual enemy targets you for persecution, trials, and tribulations. Therefore, if you're in a storm right now, it's a sign that you're on the right road. Don't say, "Oh, God, I don't know why You let this thing happen to me! God don't You know I've paid my tithes! Don't You know I've been faithful to You! I just don't understand, how You could let something like this happen to me!" Have the attitude that my God is on board my ship. I don't know why I'm in this storm, but my Lord is on my ship and He's going to take me to the other side."

God is the same yesterday, today, and forever. "Well, Pastor, I just feel so far away from God." My response is, "*God* didn't move!" His address is still the same, and He's still sitting on the same throne. If you feel far from God, guess what? *You* moved! Get back to where you are supposed to be. Start saying, "Depression, get off of me! You are not for me! Jesus is on board my ship and He's taking me to the other side."

Another thing, lighten up, and don't take life so seriously. When depression comes, you don't want to leave the house. You want to lock the door, take the phone off the hook, and wallow in self-pity. You want to whine, snivel, and cry all by yourself. "Give me a box of tissue so I can have my own pity-party." That's the worse thing you can do. Force yourself to get into church. God will change your life when you come to church. *"Not forsaking our own assembling together, as is the habit of some, but encouraging one another, and all the more, as you see the day drawing near."* (Hebrews 10:25)

You'll have to fight your feelings and your flesh, and obey what the Word of God says. Get out of the house, go to a funny movie, or go to an amusement park and get on the roller coaster! Get in the front car, strap yourself in tightly, and fly over that first hill. You'll forget all about your depression! Make up your mind that you're **NOT** going to live with depression in your life anymore. You must rise above depression and the lies of the enemy, who told you that your life is hopeless, and you have no reason to live.

Learn to laugh at yourself! Laugh at the person you're married to! You have to put some joy back in your life. Quit taking life so serious. God made us to enjoy life! *"...we are more than conquerors through Him (Christ Jesus) that loves us!"* (Romans 8:37) Your flesh will tell you to isolate yourself. Don't do it! It will destroy you. You need to be with friends and get into church. However, there are some friends you will need to stay away from, especially if you're feeling down. There are some people who will bring you right down into the pit; because that's where they are, and misery loves company!

If you're born-again, "born of God," then you are made to be an overcomer. Not every person is born-of-God, but if you are in Jesus Christ, then you are born-of-God. I don't care what religion has told you, not all roads lead to God! There is *one way* to God and that's through the Blood of His Son who died for you. His name is Jesus Christ. If your life has been destroyed, Jesus will help you, as you call on Him.

"For whatever is born of God overcomes the world; and this is the victory that has overcome the world, - our faith. And who is the one who overcomes the world, but he who believes that Jesus is the Son of God." (I John 5:4)

Denominations are not the way to God. **Jesus is the Way.** Religion isn't the way to God. **Jesus is the way to God.** No matter what difficulty you are in, or trials and tribulations you face in your life; if you are born-of-God and Jesus is your Savior, then you are made to overcome. The Word says, *"For nothing will be impossible with God."* (Luke 1:37)

Anytime you feel hopeless, depression can come in. I don't care who you are or what your name is, what label you wear, or what you call yourself; if you allow hopelessness to come into your life, then depression will follow. *Hopelessness* is not for the child of God. You are a child of the living God, not a dead god. You must remember this trial is only temporary. *"...in due season we will reap, if we faint not."* (Galatians 6:9) God will take you on to victory.

God is so **big**, He will turn every bad situation for your good. Philippians 4:13 says, *"I can do all things through Him who strengthens me."* If the Word says, *"I can do all things...,"* whether I feel like I can or not, *I can* defeat depression. If I can do all things, then I can rise above the storms in my life. I can't do it in myself, I have to have His help through Jesus living in me. Depression says, "I'm defeated, I might as well quit." Faith says, "My God loves me, and He's going to turn it *all* for my good." The Word of God says **"it came to pass."** That means *it didn't come to stay.* When you serve the Most High God, everything is subject to change!

God didn't make you to sink, but to swim. He didn't make you to be the *tail*. He made you to be the *head*. *"And the Lord shall make you the head, and not the tail; and you shall be above only...."* (Deuteronomy 28:13) We are not children of *beggars*, we are children of the *Most High God*. We are joint heirs with The *King of Kings*, and *The Lord of Lords!*

If you are feeling depressed or discouraged today, if life holds no meaning for you, then Jesus is your answer. He is the **"lighthouse in a dark land,"** and He will bring you to victory, eventually, if you will call on His name. If you want to be rid of depression, bow your head and pray this prayer.

Prayer For Healing And Restoration

Dear Heavenly Father, I thank you that you sent Your Son, Jesus to die on the Cross as my substitute. Father, I repent of *all* sin in my life, and for *all* the negative words I have spoken out of my mouth. Please change my heart and my attitude. I ask you to wash me clean with the precious Blood of Jesus Christ. I now understand that many are the afflictions of the righteous, but You will deliver ME out of *all* of them. I believe that You have a great plan for my life. Jesus, I will no longer walk by what I see. I determine in my heart today to give You the sacrifice of praise. I thank you for delievering me out of the bondage of discouragement and depression. In Jesus Name, I pray.

AMEN

Overcoming Depression

Perhaps, you are acquainted with someone who suffers from depression. Pastor Dennis Leonard's anointed teachings on this subject, are now available in book, video or cassette tapes.

Books
You Can Forgive Yourself
Overcoming Depression
Overcoming Fear
Overcoming Low Self-esteem
Overcoming Rejection

Books $5.00 each
(postage and handling included)

Video Tapes Available
($12.00 postage and handling included)

Cassette Tapes

Building A Strong Marriage
Character And Integrity
Character And Integrity - Part 2
Faith Working Through Love
Forgiveness Or Torment
Forgiving Yourself
Giving Up Control
God Will Restore The Hearts Of The Fathers
God's Supercharger
Gossip
Grace Upon Grace
Healing The Bruised
Healing The Rejected
How To Confront Others
Judge Not
Love Does Not Get Offended
Maturing Thru Confrontation
My Family Shall Be Saved
Obey God And Live
Overcoming Depression - Part 1
Overcoming Depression - Part 2
Overcoming Grasshopper Mentality - Part 1
Overcoming Grasshopper Mentality - Part 2
Raising Children
Saved By Grace Not Works
The Healing Of Your Past
The Miracle Jesus
The Name That's Above Every Name
The New Age And Antoher Jesus
The Unpardonable Sin
Tearing Down The Walls Of Unforgiveness
Using Faith For Finances
What Would Love Do
Which Sin Is Worse
You Are Valuable To God

Cassette Tapes $5.00 Each
(Postage And Handling Including)

Tape Series Available

THE BLOOD OF JESUS	4 Pack	$14.00
BRING ON THE JOY	4 Pack	$14.00
FORGIVENESS	4 Pack	$14.00
GRACE	6 Pack	$20.00
GROWING UP IN CHRIST	6 Pack	$20.00
HEALING	6 Pack	$20.00
THE HOLY SPIRIT	6 Pack	$20.00
JESUS	4 Pack	$14.00
LOVE	6 Pack	$20.00
THE LAST DAYS	6 Pack	$20.00
MARRIAGE & THE FAMILY	6 Pack	$20.00
MOUNTAIN MOVING FAITH	6 Pack	$20.00
OVERCOMING DEPRESSION	4 Pack	$14.00
OVERCOMING FEAR	4 Pack	$14.00
OVERCOMING REJECTION	6 Pack	$20.00
SEX AND CHRISTIANITY	3 Pack	$11.00
SPIRITUAL WARFARE	4 Pack	$14.00

If you wish to purchase any of Pastor Dennis Leonard's teaching materials please place your order by writing or calling Dennis Leonard Publications at the location listed below.

VISA or MasterCard orders are welcome.

Dennis Leonard Publications
1301 South Clinton Street
Denver, Colorado 80231
(303) 369-8514